Andrea Yousif

Where did baby go?

Illustrated by Olena Rii
Edited by Courtney Flowers

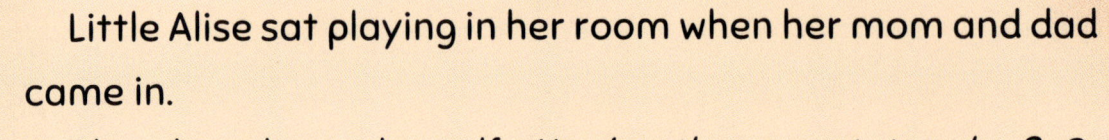

Little Alise sat playing in her room when her mom and dad came in.

She thought to herself, *Maybe they want to play? Or maybe they are going to take me to get that cold sweet icy creamy stuff. Hmm,* Alise thought, *I hope it's the icy creamy stuff!*

But when she looked at them, they seemed to be glowing as they smiled at her. She thought, *It can't be icy creamy stuff. Maybe we're going on a trip outside?*

Her parents leaned down and handed Alise a present.

"A present!" Alise yelled with joy. "I LOVE presents! But why?" she asked. "It's not my birthday. Is it Christmas time already?" Her parents laughed and said "Nope." They told her to open it.

All these thoughts raced through Alise's mind. *What could it be?? A Puppy? The talking doll I wanted? Ooooh maybe it's shoes, mine look dirty and old,* she thought, wiggling her toes through her shoes.

She tore the paper off and ripped open the tissue. *A shirt! YAY! A shirt!* Wait, do I need a shirt? She looked at her parents with confused excitement. She didn't get it. "Read it!" her parents said, with just as much excitement!

She turned the shirt every which way so that she could try to read the print. She was just learning to read. So she was putting sounds together "B-I-G S-I-I-I-S-TER, Big Sister!" she tried to sound out. *What? What does that mean?* She looked at her parents with confusion. Her parents explained to Alise that they were going to have a baby! And she would be the baby's big sister!

Alise had never had such a feeling of excitement come over her. The first thing she thought was, *Yes! I have a doll now! A REAL LIVE DOLL. Oh, I'm so happy. I'm going to feed it, wash it, and help it get dressed.* Oh, Alise couldn't wait!

Alise looked at her parents and screamed. "Now?! When is baby coming? I need to get ready." Her mom gently rubbed her stomach and said, "Oh, not for a while. You'll have plenty of time to get ready."

For the next few days, all that Alise could think about was this baby. *Wow, a baby.* She sat. She thought. She giggled. She screamed. She danced. And she had many questions for mom...

How? Why? What? Her mom lovingly tried to answer all the questions she had.

Everyday was like a dream for Alise. Every few days she would go to her mom and ask, "Today?" "No," laughed her mom. Alise got tired of waiting for this baby. What is taking so long, she asked herself. *Helloooo, we've got things to do! Play, eat, talk, sing, dance and play again.*

"Today?"

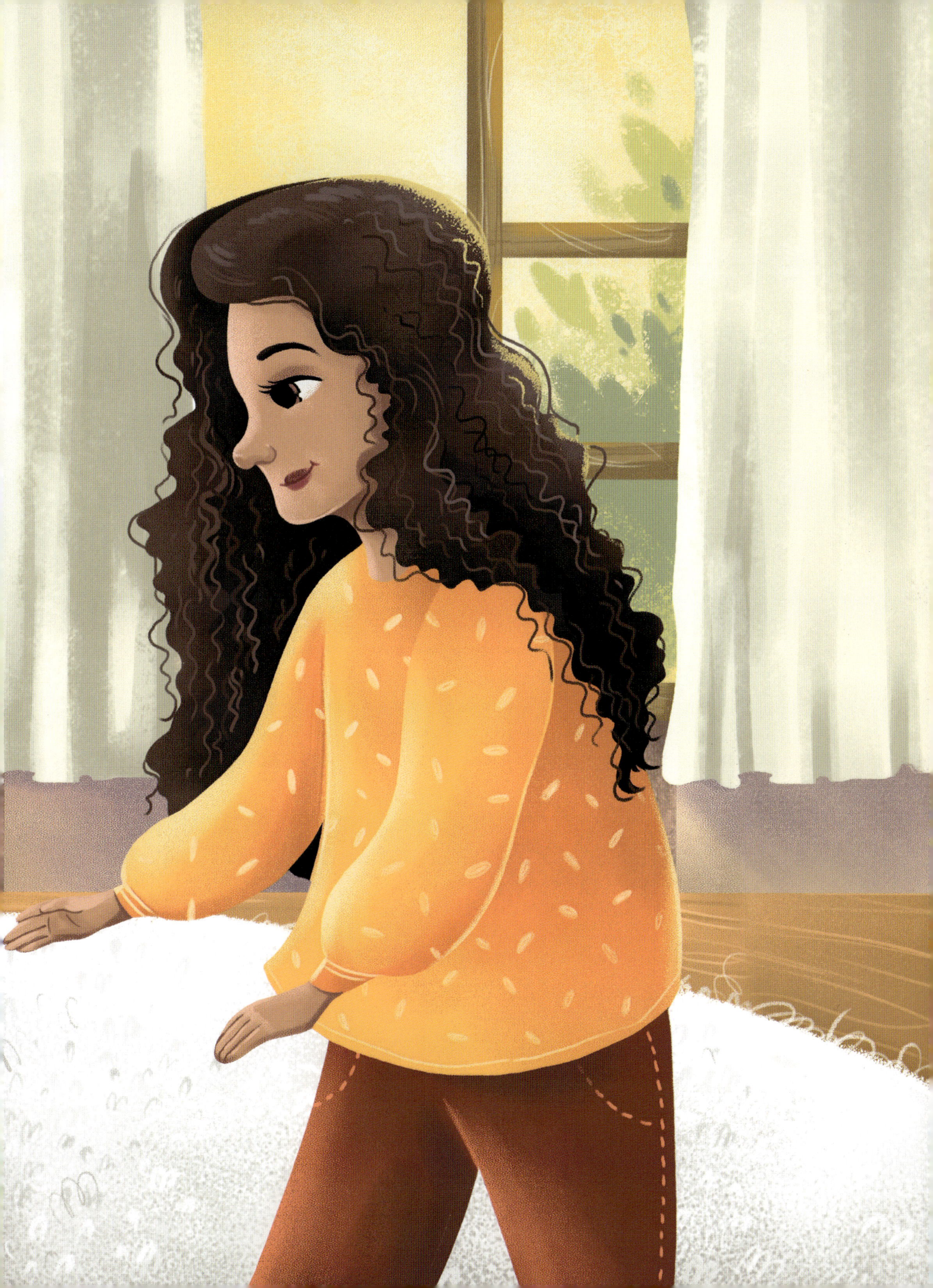

Some time went by, and one day she heard a noise coming from her parents room. It sounded like a scary, loud, sad, screaming noise. She was scared to check so she yelled out, "Mommy!...Mommy?!" She slowly but bravely walked closer to her parents room.

It sort of sounded like her mom, but what were all these noises she was making? She slowly peeked one eye into the room. Then both. She saw her mom crying, but not just a little cry, the biggest cry she'd ever seen from a big person. Her first thought was, *Oh no, mommy has an owie! I can give her a hug.*

So Alise walked to her mom and said, "Mommy it's ok, don't cry. What happened, Mommy?" She patted her mom on the leg, trying to help the way Mommy had helped her in the past.

Her mom was so, so sad. Alise thought, *I've never seen Mommy this sad before. I wonder what happened?* She asked again, "Mommy, what happened?" Tears kept falling down her mom's face. Her mom didn't say anything for a while, and just hugged Alise.

Alise just sat there with her mom. Finally, her mom said with a broken voice, "The baby is gone."

"What? What do you mean, Mommy? Baby is gone? Why? Where? Where did baby go?" Her mom was in and out of bursts of tears. She didn't say much, just held Alise tight. Alise could tell that Mommy wasn't paying attention to her questions.

Feeling confused, hot, and very sad, she sat there thinking, *Where did baby go? Why? What happened?*

Days went by and it seemed like the entire house was different. The dog was sad. Mommy and Daddy were sad. Alise felt very sad but still didn't really understand why.

She understood that baby was gone, but she had so many questions. It seemed that Mommy was too sad to answer her questions. She didn't know what to do. So she tried to play with her toys.

People stopped by, throughout the weeks, to drop off food and gifts, even though they all looked sad. It seemed to help Mommy for a little while. Mommy and Daddy would talk often, cry, and even sometimes yell.

Alise needed to know,

Where did baby go?

Finally, one day Alise's mom came to her room and put her on her lap. Hugging Alise so tightly she said, "Honey, I love you so much and everything is going to be ok." "Mommy, what happened? Please tell me," Alise said.

With tears in her eyes, she said, "Well Alise, the baby stopped growing in Mommy's tummy." "Why?" asked Alise. Her mom said, "We don't know why. The doctors said there was no reason, but that it just stopped growing and died." "Where is it now Mommy?" Alise asked.

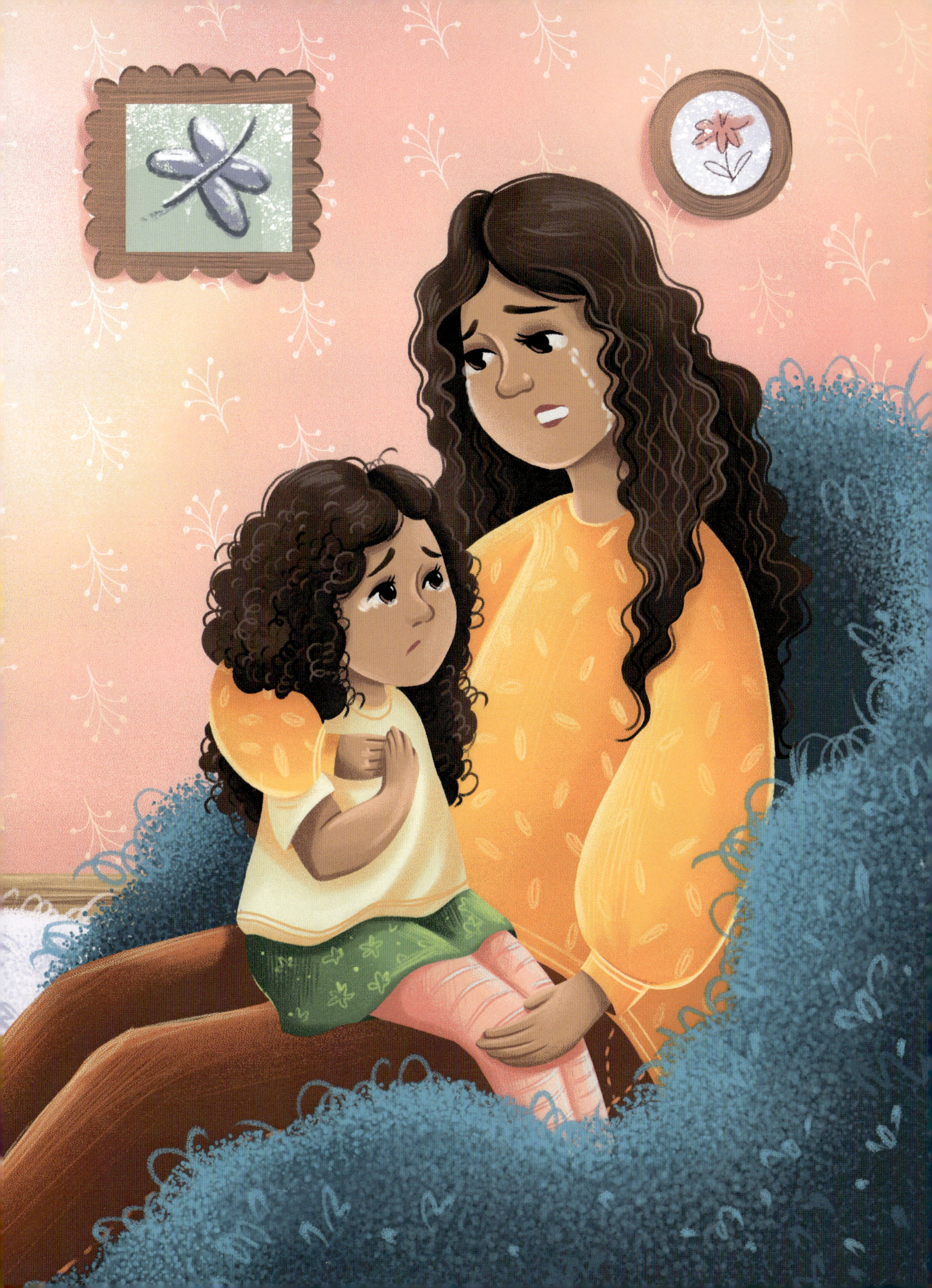

"Alise, Mommy and Daddy believe our beautiful baby is in Heaven with Jesus. I think that God chose us to be the baby's parents but He wanted to be with our baby sooner than later. The baby is safe in the arms of Jesus. One day we will meet our baby and it will be such a beautiful day." Alise's mom explained. "Are you still sad, Mommy?" asked Alise. "Yes honey, both Mommy and Daddy are still very sad. Even though we don't understand, we trust that God has a plan for us and He has a plan for our baby." Alise's mom answered.

"I'm sad, Mommy." said Alise, with crocodile tears sliding down her face. "I know, Sweetie. It's ok to be sad. We were all very excited. Some days will be hard but we still have each other. When you are sad, just come to me or Daddy and we can talk or just hug."

"Mommy, can I make something for baby?" Alise asked. "What do you mean?" her mom asked." "I want to give baby a gift." Alise replied.

Alise's mom started to cry, gently. "Yes Alise, that is a beautiful idea. I can help you, if you want."

Over the next few days Alise and her mom spent time making, writing, and creating many things for baby that were so special to them.

Alise's mom helped her write a letter, saying how much she loved and missed baby, and that she couldn't wait to meet baby up in Heaven, one day

They planted flowers, made an ornament at Christmas time, and colored many pictures for baby.

Even though losing baby was so hard for the whole family, somehow Alise felt warmer inside than before. She felt closer to her Mommy and Daddy than ever before. She felt that even though baby was gone, and they all were so sad, at least they still had each other. They were sad together and somehow it made it a little bit easier.

Alise never forgot baby, and anytime she felt sad, she would go and talk to her mom or dad about it.

Over time, laughter and joy came back into the house. They were closer as a family now, and that was a beautiful and unexpected gift that the baby had given to all of them.

Activities you can do together:

- Name your baby if you know the gender.
- Plant a Perennial flower in your garden.
- Plant a tree in your yard.
- Make a memento box: pregnancy test, medical bracelet, small notebook of their story, small toy...
- Draw a picture.
- Make a painting.
- Print an image that you want to color.
- Write the baby's story as though you would tell that baby how it came to be.
- Quill an image
- Paint/color a rock and place it in your garden/house.
- Make an ornament to hang on the Christmas Tree.
- Write a letter to the baby.
- Share your story with someone.
- Write a song.
- Write a poem.